Amazing Animals

by Judy Kentor Schmauss

 HOUGHTON MIFFLIN HARCOURT

PHOTOGRAPHY CREDITS: (c) ©Digital Vision/Getty Images; 3 (b) Corbis; 4 (b) ©Stephen Simpson/Getty Images; 5 (tl) ©James H. Robinson/Photo Researchers/Getty Images; 5 (tr) ©Alan and Sandy Carey/Photodisc/Getty Images; 5 (bl) ©Jeff Rotman/Alamy Images; 5 (br) ©Christopher Swann/Photo Researchers, Inc.; 6 (t) ©SilksAtSunrise Photography/Alamy; 7 (bl) ©Digital Vision/Getty Images; 7 (c) ©Alan and Sandy Carey/Photodisc/Getty Images; 7 (r) ©Roberta Olenick/All Canada Photos/Corbis; 8 (b) ©Christopher Swann/Photo Researchers, Inc.; 9 (t) ©Jeff Rotman/Alamy Images; 9 (b) ©J & C Sohns/age fotostock; 10 (b) © Gerry Ellis/Getty Images; 10 (t) ©Robert Shantz/Alamy Images; 10 (t) ©Photo Researchers/Getty Images; 11 (tl) ©James H. Robinson/Photo Researchers/Getty Images; 11 (tr) ©Norbert Rosing/National Geographic/Getty Images

Printed in Mexico

ISBN: 978-0-544-07236-7

4 5 6 7 8 9 10 0908 21 20 19 18 17 16 15 14

4500469985   A B C D E F G

Contents

Vocabulary

adaptation

Stretch Vocabulary

enemy

migrate

baleen

armor

Introduction

Animals live in many different places. Some live in the desert. Some animals live in the ocean. Some live in places where it is very cold.

How do animals survive in all these different places? Over many, many years, the bodies of animals like them have changed.

Why does this animal have white fur?

It Is What Is on the Outside That Counts

Like people, some animals have hearts, livers, and lungs inside their bodies.

However, on the outside, animals are different from people. They are different from each other, too.

The outside, or external, body parts of animals help them survive.

This crab has a hard outer body.

pill bug

ram

octopus

whale

You know that all animals need food and water. They also need air and a way to stay safe. Animals have adapted in different ways to their habitats so they can meet their needs.

In this book, we will look at the external body parts of some animals. You will read how some animals use these body parts to move, eat, and live.

Geese migrate in winter.

Animals on the Move

Animals in the wild are often on the move. They must find food and water. Some animals move from place to place to avoid being eaten by other animals!

Some birds migrate, or move, to another place in winter. They use their wings to fly there. Wings are adaptations that allow birds to find food.

Gibbons are small apes. They live in trees. Gibbons have very long arms. Their arms let them swing from tree to tree.

Rams live on mountains. They have split hooves with rough bottoms. Rams' hooves let them balance as they climb. Their hooves also keep them from sliding on slippery rocks.

gibbon

ram

split hoof

Time to Eat!

Adaptations allow animals to eat. Some whales have teeth. Other whales do not. They have baleen instead.

Baleen is made from the same material that our hair and nails are made from. Whales use the baleen like a strainer. The water and food go in the whale's mouth. But only the water comes out!

Baleen helps food stay in.

baleen

beak

long tongue

When you think of animals with beaks, do you think of birds? Did you know an octopus has a small beak, too? An octopus uses its eight arms to catch its prey. Then it stabs the prey with its beak.

A hungry anteater can open an anthill with its long claws. Then it licks up the ants with its tongue. Its tongue is sticky on the outside. The ants can not get away!

Everyday Living

Animals use their body parts so they can live where they do.

Chameleons are reptiles. They use adaptations to disguise themselves. Chameleons change color when their enemies get too close!

Arctic foxes are white. They blend into the ice and snow. Brown desert foxes blend into the sand.

These animals use color to hide.

chameleon

desert fox

pill bug

walrus

The outside of a pill bug looks like the armor on an armadillo. The bug can roll itself into a ball. It does this to keep from being eaten.

A walrus has a thick layer of fat under its tough hide. The fat helps keep the walrus warm.

Write a Story

Choose one of the animals you read about. Write a story. In the story, include an adventure that shows how the animal used its body and body parts to move, eat, or live. Tell your story to a friend.

Research It

Birds and some insects have wings. Look on the Internet or in books to find how the wings of birds and flies are alike. How are they different? Why are they important to the animals?